A TALKING POINTS BOOK BY
# VAUGHAN ROBERTS

# THE PORN PROBLEM

The Porn Problem
© Vaughan Roberts/The Good Book Company, 2018

**Published by**
The Good Book Company
Tel (UK): 0333 123 0880
Tel (North America): (1) 866 244 2165
International: +44 (0) 208 942 0880
Email (UK): info@thegoodbook.co.uk
Email (North America): info@thegoodbook.com

**Websites**
North America: www.thegoodbook.com
UK & Europe: www.thegoodbook.co.uk
Australia: www.thegoodbook.com.au
New Zealand: www.thegoodbook.co.nz

Unless otherwise indicated, Scripture quotations are from
The Holy Bible, New International Version, NIV Copyright © 1973,
1978, 1984, 2011 by Biblica, Inc.

ISBN: 9781784981976 | Printed in Denmark by Nørhaven

Design by André Parker

# CONTENTS

# INTRODUCTION
## TALKING POINTS

The world is changing. Fast.

And not just politics, technology and communication, but our whole culture, morality and attitudes. Christians living in Western culture have enjoyed the benefit of being in a world which largely shared our assumptions about what is fundamentally right and wrong. We can no longer assume that this is the case.

In two short generations we have moved to a widespread adoption of liberal values, many of which are in conflict with the teaching of the Bible. Increasingly, believers are finding themselves to be the misunderstood minority, and feeling at odds with where the world seems to be heading.

But let's not be blinkered: some of this change has been good. Christians have often failed to discern the difference between our own cultural values, and those that are demanded by scripture. We are as prone to bigotry as others. We have much to repent of in our attitudes towards, for example, the freedom and role of women in society, and our lack of compassion and understanding towards those who have wrestled with same-sex attraction.

But increasingly we find ourselves in unfamiliar territory and ill-equipped to deal with it. Sometimes it's easier to protest and rage against the tide of history than to go back to our Bibles and think carefully about what God is saying—holding up society's views, and our own, to the truth-revealing mirror that is God's word.

At our best, we Christians have been in the forefront of social reform. Think of the great nineteenth-century reformers of the slave trade, prisons and poverty: William Wilberforce, Elizabeth Fry, and Lord Shaftesbury. But too often, we now find ourselves on the back foot, unable to articulate a clear response to a pressing question of our day. And even when we have understood God's mind on a particular issue, we have struggled to apply it compassionately in our speech and in our relationships.

Christians are called to be wise and gentle, even when the temptation is to call out injustices and feel righteous anger. The way to approach these issues is prayerfully and to be humbly aiming to understand the culture and discern the times.

This short series of books is an attempt to help ordinary Christians start to think constructively about a range of issues—moral, ethical and cultural—that run against the grain for those who name Christ as Lord. They are an attempt to stimulate believers to start talking with each other as we search the Scriptures together. Their aim is to help us think biblically, constructively and compassionately, and not to feel intimidated when we are challenged or questioned, or, perhaps worse, remain silent. This book aims to lend perspective and to offer some biblical guidance on following God and loving people as God loves us

## WHAT THIS BOOK IS NOT...

In such a short book, we cannot hope to answer all the questions you may have about how to think about pornography—it is a complex and multifaceted issue. Nor can we address the many practical challenges you may be facing with your family or friends, or personally.

Nor have we attempted to present a thorough treatment of all the Bible has to say on these questions. If that is what you are hungry for, there are other, longer books that will help you dig deeper. You will find a list of suggestions in the further resources section at the end.

## WHAT THIS BOOK IS...

Rather, our aim is to give you an accessible introduction to the many questions that surround the issue of pornography, and a starting point for constructive discussion between Christian believers and others. We aim to give you a cultural briefing on where we are with this question, and some pointers on how Christians should think, talk and act.

But we also hope that reading this book will take you beyond the issue—to a genuine compassion and love for those who are caught up in some way with pornography; and to how we might help them see both the dangers, and how they might find help and freedom. We're also aware that this book touches on something that is deeply personal to you. Whatever your situation, our prayer is that this book will be a first step towards understanding the landscape, and an encouragement to know and share the love, hope and freedom we have in Christ.

**Tim Thornborough**
Series Editor | January 2018

# pornography

[poor-*nog*-ra-fee]

*noun*: **pornography**
printed or visual material containing the explicit
description or display of sexual organs or activity,
intended to stimulate sexual excitement.

*synonyms:* erotica, pornographic material, pornographic, soft-core pornography, dirty
books, smut, filth, vice; *informal* porn,
hard porn, soft porn, porno, skin/girlie
magazines

[Source: Google definitions]

*Porn doesn't play games, porn doesn't text back, porn … gives you exactly what you ask for. I love you porn! I love the always happy endings in porn.*
**A selection of tweets on pornography**

*There is no dignity when the human dimension is eliminated from the person. In short, the problem with pornography is not that it shows too much of the person, but that it shows far too little."* **Pope John Paul II**

*Religious people use 10% more pornography than secular people. All that religious preaching does no good.*
**Darrel Ray, psychologist and atheist activist**

*No one shuts their laptop after looking at pornography and says, "What a productive time I just spent connecting with the world!"* **Russell Brand, comedian**

*Pornography, to me, represents freedom.*
**Jenna Jamieson, porn star**

*You have heard that it was said, "You shall not commit adultery." But I tell you that anyone who looks at a woman lustfully has already committed adultery with her in his heart. If your right eye causes you to stumble, gouge it out and throw it away.* **Matthew 5 v 27-29**

*Jesus replied, "Very truly I tell you, everyone who sins is a slave to sin … if the Son sets you free, you will be free indeed."* **John 8 v 34, 36**

# THE PORN PROBLEM

## CHAPTER ONE

There has always been pornography of some kind or another—erotic depictions in art, sculpture and on pottery have been discovered in virtually every ancient culture. In some cultures and eras, its availability, acceptability and use have been widespread. At other times, it has been repressed, legislated against and driven underground. But something very dramatic has happened in the last 20 years or so. We've seen a monumental explosion of porn, sparked by the "triple-A engine" of cyber sex: *Accessibility*, *Affordability* and *Anonymity*.[1]

When I was a teenager, if you wanted to get hold of porn you had to risk the embarrassment of being seen reaching for the shelf on the magazine rack that

---

1 Al Cooper, *Cybersex: The Dark Side of the Force* (Brunner-Routledge, 2000), p 2.

was probably too high for you anyway. And you'd have to dig into your pocket and pay some real money. What a difference today! There is complete anonymity. In the privacy of your own home, wherever you have your laptop or phone, there is porn on demand, free to view.

And vast numbers of people are consuming it. The highly respected Nielsen Media Research organisation reported that about 60 million people—over a quarter of internet users in the United States—visited a pornographic website during one month in 2010.[2] In case you believe the myth that it's almost exclusively men who look at porn, it's worth noting that the same group revealed in one study that a third of visitors to porn sites are female.[3]

Online images are far from the only expression of porn. Erotic fiction is readily available, on the internet and in print. This has now entered the mainstream, as seen by the extraordinary success of the novel *Fifty Shades of Grey*, which by June 2015 had sold 125 million copies in just four years. Verbal descriptions, along with the images we see,

---

2 Quoted in Jonathan Grant, *Divine Sex* (Brazos Press, 2015), p 104.

3 Helen Thorne, *Purity is Possible* (The Good Book Company, 2014), p 7.

combine to feed fantasies we create for ourselves. Sometimes the most powerful porn is stuff we create in our own heads.

## GETTING THE RIGHT PERSPECTIVE

If you are someone who takes Jesus seriously, you will already suspect that viewing and reading porn, or manufacturing it ourselves in our imaginations, is something that does not fit with his teaching. He said, "I tell you that anyone who looks at a woman lustfully has already committed adultery with her in his heart" (Matthew 5 v 28).

But it's not just Christians who are worried about the tsunami of porn that has hit our society in recent years. Social commentators, medical professionals and concerned individuals point to the negative impact it is having, for example, on body image, relational health and the development of adolescent sexuality. Only time will tell what the full effect will be. One writer comments:

> *I would not be surprised if we're evolving to be a less intimate culture. Maybe it won't matter if some people struggle with intimacy and connection, because they'll have robotic devices to meet their needs ... what all this is going to mean in twenty years from now, we have no idea. We are in an evolutionary phase. Some*

*of us will survive and thrive in this new environment we've created and some of us won't. It is the greatest social experiment we have ever experienced.*[4]

## CLOSER TO HOME

I know that many who read these words won't need convincing that porn is wrong. It may be that you're a Christian who loves Jesus Christ, wants to live to please him and knows that should include keeping your heart sexually pure, but you're very conscious you haven't done that. You're not alone—that's true of all of us, including me. I am a sexual sinner writing to sexual sinners. Exactly how we have fallen short sexually will vary. Not all who read this book will have a problem with porn, but many certainly will—perhaps including you.

Porn use is usually private and therefore hidden from others. That can lead to a deep sense of shame and guilt, which leaves many people feeling alone and isolated. Perhaps you can identify with that. You feel bad about what you have done and what you keep doing, but you don't feel able to talk about it with others. And you may not even feel you can be

---

4   Interview with Robert Weiss, co-author of *Always Turned On: Facing Sexual Addiction in the Digital Age* (Gentle Path Press, 2015), in *The Sunday Times* 8 February 2015.

real with God, so there is also a damaging distance in your relationship with him.

This shame affects both sexes, but can be a particular problem for women. If porn, sexual fantasy and masturbation are ever mentioned in church circles—and all too often they aren't—it is frequently assumed that they are only an issue for men. That leaves the many women who face this battle even more inclined to keep it to themselves. Married people can also be especially affected, because of the mistaken belief that it is mainly singles who view porn. As a result they can be too ashamed to let anyone know about their struggle.

Private shame so often leads to private despair. It may be that as you read these words you have already lost hope. You know that sexual sin has got a grip on you, but you feel powerless to shake it off. I'm speaking especially about pornography, but the principles apply beyond pornography to all types of sexual sin, or indeed to sin of any kind. You've tried hundreds or thousands of times to stop and you haven't been able to, so you may even have given up trying.

If we are to help Christians who feel held by the grip of porn, we must begin by seeking to change the culture of our churches. We need to speak more openly about these issues and encourage those who struggle to be honest with trusted friends or pastors. They can then be pointed away from the darkness and lies that hold them captive towards the light and truth of Christ that can set them free.

The Bible has wonderful news for those who are beginning to feel they will never find victory in the fight against porn. The gospel of Jesus Christ offers complete forgiveness and also a new power by the Holy Spirit to enable us to fight sin and grow in holiness. It really is possible to live porn-free. Jesus is realistic about the power that sin can exert over us, but he also has a message of glorious hope for us, however low we have sunk:

> *Everyone who sins is a slave to sin ... [but] if the Son sets you free, you will be free indeed.*
> John 8 v 34, 36

# SEX AND
# GOD'S DESIGN

## CHAPTER TWO

An article in *Time* magazine a few years ago contained these striking words:

> *Of all the splendidly ridiculous, transcendentally fulfilling things humans do, it is sex ... that most confounds understanding. What in the world are we doing? Why ... are we so consumed by it? The impulse to procreate may lie at the heart of sex, but ... bursting from our sexual center is a whole spangle of other things—art, song, romance, obsession, rapture, sorrow, companionship, love, even violence and criminality ... Why should this be so? Did nature simply overload us in the mating*

*department ... ? Or is there something smarter and subtler at work, some larger interplay among sexuality, life and what it means to be human?*[5]

It's a great question. Those who have a purely materialistic worldview, which seeks to explain everything in terms of scientific processes alone, are bound to reduce sex in the end to just a biological urge—hardwired into us to ensure we reproduce. According to that understanding, now that we have reasonably safe forms of contraception, what's to stop us from satisfying our sexual urges whenever we feel like it, as long as consenting adults are involved?

You're hungry? *Have a pizza.*

You're thirsty? *Have a coke.*

You're turned on? *Have an orgasm—with another person or on your own. And if porn helps—go for it! There's nothing to it; it's just satisfying a bodily urge, that's all.*

But we instinctively sense that there's something more to sex than that. Our sexuality seems to touch us at the core of our being. So what is sex about? Could it be that the journalist is right—that it does have something to do with "what it means to be human"?

---

5  *Time*, 19 January 2004, p 64.

## SOMETHING MORE

The narrative of the sexual revolution was that the Bible's sexual ethics, and those of Christianity in general, are repressive, guilt- and shame-inducing, and totally outdated. The only option was to reject them. But when we look at the Bible, we find the very opposite. Scripture has a wonderfully high view of sex. Right from the first pages—Genesis chapter 1—we read of a God who made human beings as sexual creatures, in the image of God.

*So God created mankind in his own image,*
*in the image of God he created them;*
*male and female he created them.*

*God blessed them and said to them,*
*"Be fruitful and increase in number; fill*
*the earth and subdue it."* Genesis 1 v 27-28

Notice that the very first command that God gives to humankind is ... that they should have sex—"be fruitful and increase in number". Sex with a purpose—to populate the earth and make it fruitful!

In Genesis chapter 2, God institutes marriage as the context for this fruitful sexuality. When the man, Adam, first meets the woman, Eve, he bursts into a song of delight:

*The man said,*

*"This is now bone of my bones*
*    and flesh of my flesh;*
*she shall be called 'woman',*
*    for she was taken out of man."*

*That is why a man leaves his father and*
*mother and is united to his wife, and they*
*become one flesh.*

*Adam and his wife were both naked, and they*
*felt no shame.*                    Genesis 2 v 23-25

Adam's excited outburst is not the last love song in the Bible. In fact, the Bible contains a whole book of lyrical poems, the *Song of Songs*, in which a man and a woman speak in powerfully erotic terms of their love for one another. The Bible is certainly not prudish about the realities of sex. And notice the absence of shame in Genesis 1. There is nothing dirty or bad about sex in God's design. Adam and Eve enjoy complete intimacy without fear or guilt.

There is delight and excitement. And inherent in this story is the truth that sex is not simply for my appetite and my desires. Its purpose is for something much deeper and more profound that requires the uniting of the two in an unbreakable marriage bond. Sex is for pleasure, yes, but it also operates as a kind of glue that binds a couple together in their lifelong, one-flesh union. And it's in that context that children are to be born: within the committed relationship of their parents.

You might say that sex is the body language of lifelong commitment.

We're all familiar with body language. You shake someone's hand; it's an expression of friendship. You kiss them on the cheek; it's an expression of affection. You have sex with them and you are saying—at least you're meant to be saying—"I love you and I am completely committed to you for life". That's God's design. Sex is not simply *recreational*; it is profoundly *relational*.

## INSTINCTIVE

Deep down we all know this. I think of a man who admitted to me that he lived a promiscuous lifestyle. And then he added, very honestly, "You know, every time I have sex with someone I leave something of myself behind".

He realised that sex is meant to be deeply inter-personal. It includes the soul; it's not just a physical thing. This explains why porn can never satisfy us. Our sexual desires are not just a longing for a physical sensation. Ultimately, we are not simply craving an orgasm or a moment of intimate connection with another person; we are yearning for a deep union with another person, not just physically, but at every level of our being.

So God is certainly not being a killjoy when he tells us to keep sex within marriage. He's our loving Creator, who knows what's best for us; it's always wise to live according to the Maker's instructions. All the Bible's negatives about sex follow from the positive teaching about sex and marriage in Genesis 1 and 2. God wants to protect his good gift of sex and he wants to protect us too. Porn, which is by its nature selfish and unrelational, not only demeans sex; *it also harms us*. We'll return to this thought in the next chapter.

## ULTIMATE MEANING

But our sexuality, in God's good design, is not just intended to bind a man and a woman together in marriage. There's something else going on, which takes us even deeper: to the very meaning and purpose of our lives.

C.S. Lewis articulates this with deep insight in his autobiography *Surprised by Joy*. He describes his early life, when he pursued sexual encounters:

> *I repeatedly followed that path—to the end. And at the end one found pleasure; which immediately resulted in the discovery that pleasure was not what you had been looking*

> *for. No moral question was involved; I was at this time as nearly nonmoral on that subject as a human creature can be. The frustration did not consist in finding a "lower" pleasure instead of a "higher." It was the irrelevance of the conclusion that marred it ... You might as well offer a mutton chop to a man who is dying of thirst as offer sexual pleasure to the desire I am speaking of ... Joy is not a substitute for sex; sex is very often a substitute for Joy. I sometimes wonder whether all pleasures are not substitutes for Joy.*[6]

The story of the Bible proclaims the fact that sex and marriage point beyond themselves to something even more wonderful, which is the "joy" that C.S. Lewis is referring to. The Bible begins with human marriage in Genesis 2, but it ends with the marriage of Christ and the church in Revelation 21 when, at the end of time, Christ and his people will be joined together in perfect intimacy. The former is a trailer of the latter. The marriage of a man and a woman is designed as a picture of a relationship with God, which he offers to us all through Christ.

Paul makes this explicit in Ephesians 5 v 32. Having quoted the Bible's foundational words about human marriage in Genesis 2 v 24, he adds:

---

6  C.S. Lewis, *Surprised by Joy* (Geoffrey Bles, 1955), p. 161.

> *This is a profound mystery—but I am talking about Christ and the church.*[7]

So our sexual longings point even beyond a desire for union with another person. At the deepest level they bear witness to a spiritual desire for connection with the God who made us in his image to relate to him. That explains why even the best sexual experience and the closest marriage will never completely fulfil us. But one day, when Christ returns, all our longings will be finally and fully satisfied for ever.

---

7  This is why marriage in the Bible is between a man and a woman and not two people of the same sex: "For marriage to be a parable of Christ and the church, it must be between like and unlike—male and female. Change this arrangement, and you end up distorting the spiritual reality to which it points. Alter marriage, and you end up distorting a picture of the gospel itself." (Sam Allberry, "How Celibacy Can Fulfil Your Sexuality", The Gospel Coalition website, 26 August 2016. Accessed 11 August 2017.)

# THE UGLINESS
# OF PORN

## CHAPTER THREE

When the journalist Malcolm Muggeridge was living in India as a young man, he wrote to his father to describe an incident that happened as he was swimming in a river. He saw a woman in the distance:

> She came to the river and took off her clothes and stood naked, her brown body just caught by the sun. I suddenly went mad. There came to me that dryness in the back of my throat; that feeling ... of wild unreasonableness which is called passion. I darted with all the force of swimming I had to where she was, and then nearly fainted, for she was old and hideous and her feet were deformed and turned inwards and her skin was wrinkled and, worst of all, she was a leper ... [u]ntil you have seen one

*you do not know the worst that human ugliness can be. This creature grinned at me, showing a toothless mask, and the next thing I knew was that I was swimming along in my old way in the middle of the stream—yet trembling ... It was the kind of lesson I needed. When I think of lust now I think of this lecherous woman.*[8]

Porn is like that. It can appear to be irresistibly attractive, but we don't have to look for long to discover that this is only a deceptive veneer. It promises delicious, nourishing fruit, but the sweetness quickly turns sour.

We soon find that what had appeared beautiful is in fact very ugly indeed—very different from the wonder of sex in God's design.

## PORN CHEAPENS SEX

Sex in porn is entirely physical, with the performers only relating sexually. And, of course, those who view them have no relationship with them. It's an entirely selfish activity which is all about me: my fantasies, my appetites. I'm in control. I can get exactly what I want, when I want. That is a sad per-

---

8  Ian Hunter, *Malcolm Muggeridge: A Life* (Harper Collins, 1980), p 40-41, cited in Douglas Sean O'Donnell, *The Song of Solomon: An Invitation to Intimacy* (Crossway, 2012), p 75-76.

version of God's good design for sex which is meant to be, as Tim Chester puts it…

> the celebration and climax—quite literally— of a relationship … If you view sex as personal gratification or a chance to enact your fantasy … then that sex will be bad in both senses of the word: poor quality and ungodly.[9]

## PORN OBJECTIFIES PEOPLE

Porn not only demeans sex; it also cheapens people. In porn the other person is just a body on a screen. The pictures don't invite us to ask questions about the real person: "Are they married? Do they have children? and, "Why are they doing this?" In the images the participants seem happy and willing.

That is part of the fantasy that porn wants to project. There are plenty of performers in "the adult industry" who would defend it, but you don't have to look far to discover a darker side. On a website which shares the stories of those who have left the industry, one woman writes:

> Like most porn performers, I perpetuated this lie. One of my favorite things to say when asked if I liked doing a particular scene was, "I only do what I like!" … What a total lie! I did

---

9   Tim Chester, *Captured by a Better Vision* (IVP, 2010) p 23.

*what I had to do to get "work" in porn. I did
what I knew would help me gain "fame" in the
industry.*[10]

Martin Daubney was the editor of *Loaded* from
2003 to 2010—a magazine that defined the laddish
culture of the time. His perspective on the images of
naked women that he published changed when he
became a father. He wrote:

*I started seeing the women in my magazine not
as sexual objects but as somebody's daughter . . .
it was almost heartbreaking."* [11]

## PORN DAMAGES SELF-ESTEEM

Viewing porn can lead us to objectify not just the
individuals on the screen, but also people more
generally. It encourages us to focus on the body
rather than on the whole person. That can in turn
affect how we see ourselves. It's no wonder that
many feel inadequate when they compare themselves to the perfectly formed bodies on the screen.
The American Psychological Association has stated,
"The saturation of sexualised images of females is

---

10 "10 Popular Ex-Porn Stars Share the Raw Reality Behind
Their Most Popular Scenes", Fight the New Drug (website),
2 January 2017. Accessed 21 September 2017.

11 *Daily Mail*, 8 June 2012.

leading to body hatred, eating disorders, low self-esteem [and] depression".[12]

It is certainly not just women and girls who feel these pressures. Many boys and men have deep concerns about their bodies and, for an increasing number, this is leading to problems that require medical attention. It used to be that those who were afflicted by eating disorders were almost entirely women, but the number of male sufferers has been rising steadily.[13]

## PORN HARMS THE YOUNG

As porn has become more accessible, increasing numbers of children are viewing it at a very young age. Much of their sex education is through discovery online. And they're not just learning the facts of life through porn; it's also forming their attitudes to sex and their understanding of what is normal sexually.

Martin Daubney, who had argued, when he was

---

12 Quoted in Tim Chester, p 26. A recent BBC programme re-vealed that girls as young as nine are seeking surgery on their genitals. It quoted a doctor as saying that they are feeling pressured by the unrealistic images they are seeing through porn and social media. (Victoria Derbyshire programme, 3 July 2017. Accessed 7 July 2017.)

13 Ed Brooks and Pete Nicholas, *Virtually Human* (IVP, 2015), p 131. They also note that in the UK in 2014 there were 1.6 million sufferers, of whom 11% were male (p. 131).

editor of *Loaded*, that porn wasn't harmful, completely changed his view as he did research for a TV documentary. Having seen the way in which so many young lives have been damaged, he concluded:

> *I feel as if an entire generation's sexuality has been hijacked by grotesque online porn.*[14]

Evidence backs up his claim.

> *In a recent survey of 16 to 18-year-old Americans, nearly every participant reported learning how to have sex by watching porn, and many of the young women said they were pressured to play out the "scripts" their male partners had learned from porn. They felt badgered into having sex in uncomfortable positions, faking sexual responses, and consenting to unpleasant or painful acts.*[15]

## PORN CORRUPTS ITS USERS

The more you watch porn, the more desensitised you become to it. The more you see, the less it arouses you; and so you'll be tempted to go deeper in to get the same hit.

---

14 *Daily Mail*, 25 September 2013. Accessed 8 August 2017.

15 "How Porn Can Hurt Your Partner", Fight the New Drug, 4 May 2017. Accessed 9 May 2017.

And, of course, the porn industry also does all it can to lead you down that path with pop-up adverts and enticing glimpses. The result is often a progression towards more extreme images, so you end up in places you never imagined you'd go—and having gone once, it's so much easier to return.[16]

In a survey of 1,500 young men, 56% admitted that their tastes in porn had become "increasingly extreme or deviant".[17] And research suggests that the impact is not limited to behaviour online: a peer-reviewed research study that analysed data from seven different countries concluded that there is "little doubt that, on average, individuals who consume pornography more frequently are more likely to hold attitudes [supporting] sexual aggression and engage in actual acts of sexual aggression".[18]

## PORN TURNS PEOPLE IN ON THEMSELVES

Augustine of Hippo, the early-church thinker, had an interesting definition for sin. He called it "love

---

16 Child pornography is, of course, illegal. If you suspect that someone you know may be looking at such images, or if this is a temptation for you, specialist advice is available at www. stopitnow.org.uk.

17 Quoted in "How Porn Affects your Sexual Tastes", Fight the New Drug, 4 May 2017. Accessed 9 May 2017.

18 "How Porn Affects Your Sexual Tastes", Fight the New Drug, 4 May 2017. Accessed 9 May 2017.

turned in on itself". We were made to be people who loved God, and who loved other people, but we turned that love in on ourselves, to our ruin.

That's exactly what's going on with porn. C.S. Lewis describes how sexual fantasy takes the sexual appetite, which is meant to lead to deep connection with another, and "turns it back: sending the man back into the prison of himself, there to keep a harem of imaginary brides". Of course, the same process happens in the imaginations of many women as well. Lewis continues:

> *This harem, once admitted, works against his **ever** getting out and really uniting with a real woman. For the harem is always accessible, always subservient, calls for no sacrifices or adjustments, and can be endowed with erotic and psychological attractions which no real woman can rival. Among those shadowy brides, he is always adored, always the perfect lover: no demand is made on his unselfishness, no mortification ever imposed on his vanity. In the end, they become merely a medium through which he increasingly adores himself.[19]*

---

19 Letter from C.S. Lewis to Keith Masson, June 3, 1956. Quoted in Jonathan Grant, *Divine Sex*, p 111.

This can be a particular problem for young people, especially those who have grown up spending a great deal of time online, much of it in gaming and watching porn. As a result, they are kept in a loop of instant gratification. That is much easier than making the effort of trying to connect with real people in the offline world. One teenager said, "Who needs the hassle of dating when I've got online porn?"[20] But porn doesn't just impact single people; it also has a profound effect on those who are married.

## PORN UNDERMINES MARRIAGE

Research suggests that the majority of those who have compulsive porn habits are married men.[21] Every time a married person of either sex looks at porn, they are committing adultery in their heart. That in itself damages intimacy, as does the secrecy involved in porn use. There is also an impact, of course, when a partner finds out that their spouse has been watching porn.

Common reactions include a sense of rejection, jealousy, anger, humiliation and loss of trust. It can also lead to a feeling of inadequacy. The feminist writer Naomi Wolf expresses how many women feel:

20 Quoted in Jonathan Grant, *Divine Sex*, p 113.

21 Al Cooper *et al*, quoted in Jonathan Grant, *Divine Sex*, p 109.

*How can a real woman—with pores and her own breasts and even sexual needs of her own ... possibly compete with a cybervision of perfection, downloadable and extinguishable at will, who comes, so to speak, utterly submissive and tailored to the consumer's least specification?* [22]

## PORN UNDERMINES FUTURE MARRIAGES

Perhaps you're thinking, "I'm single so I needn't worry about watching porn, as I'm not hurting anyone else. This is a temporary way of dealing with my sexual desires, but as soon as marriage comes along, I'll have sex instead with a real person."

But don't assume that you'll be able to stop once you're married—habits formed over a long period are not easily kicked. And, even if you do stop, there will still be an impact from the porn you have watched in the past, not just because of the images that linger in the brain, but perhaps physically as well.

An article on the website Fight the New Drug describes a disturbing reality:

*Every time someone consumes porn, especially if they heighten the experience by masturbating,*

---

[22] "The Porn Myth", *New York Magazine*, 20 October 2003. Accessed 1 August 2017.

*the part of the brain map that connects arousal to porn is being strengthened. Meanwhile, the pathways connecting arousal to things like seeing, touching, or cuddling with a partner aren't getting used. Pretty soon, natural turn-ons aren't enough, and many porn consumers find they can't get aroused by anything but porn.*[23]

This is contributing to a rapid increase in erectile dysfunction among younger men—a problem which, until recently, almost always only affected men over the age of 40. It's a sad irony that, as a result of having gone to porn to seek sexual fulfilment, these men become incapable of the very thing they were pursuing.

Ironically, the problem with porn is that it shows not too much, *but too little*. Because it focuses on the physical and the visible, it completely misses the far greater and more wonderful thing that God has given to us. Porn does not show us the joy of human love and commitment; the deep nurturing satisfaction of two people made one flesh; the fulfilment and fruitfulness of two lives lived together to the glory of God; and the nurture of a family. Porn

23 "How Porn Damages Your Sex Life", *Fight the New Drug*, 4 May 2017. Accessed 9 May 2017.

is the equivalent of burning a priceless Stradivarius violin for a few moments of warmth, and missing out on a lifetime of beautiful, glorious music.

And by setting the bar, and our expectations, so low, it impoverishes and demeans us all.

This is not freedom; it's slavery.

# THE SLAVERY OF PORN

## CHAPTER FOUR

**M**any people don't need convincing of the ugliness of porn. They've seen and felt it in society at large, in someone close to them, or in their own life. And yet that doesn't stop lots of them—and perhaps you—from continuing to go back to it. Many recognise that there's a compulsive element to their porn use; what promised freedom has enslaved them. They can echo Paul's words:

> *I do not understand what I do. For what I want to do I do not do, but what I hate I do.*
>
> Romans 7 v 15

Why is this?

### SINFUL HEARTS

Perhaps we think to ourselves that the problem of porn is largely external to us. We imagine that if only those porn sites could be shut down, or we managed to get all the right filters on our devices, we'd be fine. If only erotic fiction and provocative images on advertising boards and in magazines could be banned, then we wouldn't struggle with lust. But, however helpful those steps might be, they won't deal with the problem because, at root, its source is not anything outside ourselves. Jesus said:

> *What comes out of a person is what defiles them. For it is from within, out of a person's heart, that evil thoughts come—sexual immorality, theft, murder, adultery, greed, malice, deceit, lewdness, envy, slander, arrogance and folly. All these evils come from inside and defile a person.* Mark 7 v 20-23

We can be quick to blame our behaviour on other factors: our sexualised culture and the easy availability of porn, the corrupting influence of others or the scars of damage done in early life. Perhaps those things have played their part, but we have to face up to the fact that the fundamental reason why we look at porn is because of our corrupt hearts.

We'll never make real progress in the battle against porn unless we recognise that, first and foremost, we are not victims; we are perpetrators. We are sinners.

## WHAT'S THE FUEL?

It's only once we have recognised that the real problem is our sin that we are ready to consider what else may be going on when we look at porn. The explanation may well not be as simple as lust alone.

John Mayer the musician has been starkly self-revealing in media interviews, speaking openly, among other things, about his fantasies, porn use and sexual lifestyle. In one interview, he describes himself as a "self-soother".[24] He continues:

> *I don't [masturbate] because I'm horny ... No I do it because I want to take a brain bath. It's like a hot whirlpool for my brain.*[25]

That, I think, is true for many. The temptation to look at porn is often not driven just by sexual drives. Very often there's another trigger: the desire for "a brain bath" perhaps. Lust could be the spark, but the fuel may come from another source. So it may be worth asking, "What's the fuel for me?" Is there a deeper motivation that gives potency to our lust?

Is it a longing for intimacy or control? What are you medicating? Is it low self-image—or a sense that people are looking down on you so you feel small and

---

24 Jonathan Grant, *Divine Sex*, p 83.

25 Quoted in Erik Hedegaard, "The Dirty Mind and Lonely Heart of John Mayer", *Rolling Stone*, 6 June 2012.

unimportant? Or perhaps you feel that no one loves you—and porn seems to take those negative emotions away. When you wrap yourself in the cocoon of your fantasies and experience the adrenalin rush that porn can bring, you can leave the harsh world of reality behind, with the hurtful feelings it generates. Instead, you can enter a world in which you're the hero, the person who is admired and desired; the one who is in complete control. It's your own personal movie into which you can escape whenever you want.

## A DIFFERENT MEDICINE

I hope you recognise how spiritually catastrophic this is—because we should be taking those feelings to a different doctor, with a different medicine. We should be taking them to the Lord Jesus Christ— because he alone is the one who can satisfy our deepest longings.

*You don't feel loved?* He loves you more than you can even begin to understand.

> *I have loved you with an everlasting love; I*
> *have drawn you with unfailing kindness.*
> Jeremiah 31 v 3

*You feel out of control?* He overrules every detail, not just of your life, but of the whole of the world. That means you can trust him absolutely.

*Are not two sparrows sold for a penny? Yet not one of them will fall to the ground outside your Father's care. And even the very hairs of your head are all numbered. So don't be afraid; you are worth more than many sparrows.*

Matthew 10 v 29-31

*You feel looked down on, as though no one likes you?* Jesus knows your sin and yet he still wants to lift you up.

*He raises the poor from the dust and lifts the needy from the ash heap; he seats them with princes and makes them inherit a throne of honour.* 1 Samuel 2 v 8

But if we have got into the rut of instinctively looking in the direction of porn when bad feelings come, the real problem is masked. And so very likely we think to ourselves, "I've got a lust problem". But we fail to recognise that underneath something deeper is going on, that we're not really addressing; so we never take it to Jesus to medicate, even though he's the best doctor.

Ironically, whatever we're trying to medicate keeps getting worse because in the end, we don't feel better. The film quickly stops and we have to return to reality, where the world doesn't revolve around us and where we're not as loved as we'd like to be. We go looking for intimacy, but end up feeling more isolated. We want to feel in control, but feel more helpless than ever. And, because of our sense of shame, we're even less inclined to look to the only one who can really help us. At that point the pull of porn, with its promise of escape, becomes very powerful again. That can so easily lead to binges and a spiral into addictive patterns. As we'll see, there is a bio-psychological explanation for sexual addictions, but there is also a profoundly spiritual element to them.

## ADDICTION

There is no doubt about the ability of porn to ensnare those who watch and use it. Psychologists describe as addicted those who spend at least 11 or 12 hours a week searching for or watching pornographic material, although many spend two or three times that amount of time on the hunt.

Typically, addictive porn use, like other forms of addiction, reaches the point where it interferes with healthy activities, resulting in relationship, career, health, financial and legal troubles.

Common signs that casual porn use has escalated to the level of addiction include:

- continued porn use despite promising yourself and others that you will stop

- increasing the amount of time spent on porn use
- needing to increase the intensity or type of sexual content viewed in order to get a fix
- lying about and covering up the nature and extent of porn use
- anger or irritability if asked to stop
- loss of interest in sexual relationships with spouses or partners
- feeling alone or detached from others
- using drugs or alcohol in conjunction with porn
- objectifying strangers, or viewing them as body parts rather than people[26]

Sadly, porn addicts are often reluctant to seek help because they don't view their solo sexual behaviours as a cause of their life problems. When they do reach out, they often seek help, not for the porn problem itself, but for the symptoms of the problem, such as depression or relationship issues.

Many participate in therapy for a long time without ever bringing up (or being asked about) pornography, and so their core problem goes unidentified and unaddressed. Sadly, this is not just a problem outside the church, but also affects Christian believers.

---

26 This list has been adapted from www.sexualrecovery.com/pornography-addiction/. Accessed 3 April 2017.

Even if they would not be formally defined as addicted, most regular porn users know the powerful pull of porn. Many studies have shown that it can have a profound bio-psychological effect.[27] Watching porn triggers the release of dopamine, a chemical which gives a kind of pleasure kick. The more you have of it, the more you want to have. And, as you keep going back for more, you end up reinforcing a brain pathway which becomes more and more instinctive to use—and increasingly hard to escape from. This condition can leave people feeling trapped, but there is hope.

A neuroscientist was asked by a friend of mine if the process that leads to this programming of the brain's demands is reversible. He replied with an emphatic "yes". He said, "Like a spoiled child that demands sweets all the time—you can retrain it." When my friend asked how, he responded, "Stop giving in to its demands—sooner or later it will stop demanding."[28]

But resisting porn's demands is easier said than done. Deep and lasting change will never come by our effort alone. Remember, the fundamental

---

27 See, for example, William M. Struthers, *Wired for Intimacy: How Pornography Hijacks the Male Brain* (IVP, 2009).

28 Simon Ponsonby, *Different* (Hodder & Stoughton 2016), p 126.

problem that causes slavery to porn is not our psychology or biology, but our sin. And to counter that, we can't rely on self-help. We need a saviour. Only Jesus Christ can truly set us free.

# TRUE FREEDOM
## CHAPTER FIVE

The message of the sexual revolution is that Christianity enslaves and represses people, while sexual licence sets them free. But the reality is exactly the opposite. Christ brings freedom, not slavery; and that includes freedom from the guilt and grip of porn.

### A HUGE GULF

The Bible is clear that all of us, without exception, are sinners:

> *There is no one righteous, not even one.*
>
> Romans 3 v 10

> *All have sinned and fall short of the glory of God.*
>
> Romans 3 v 23

That's important to remember as we read a book like this. It may be that porn isn't a problem for you.

You don't look at it and you may even be disgusted at the thought of those who do. If so, you need to heed the Bible's warnings against self-righteousness:

> *You … have no excuse, you who pass*
> *judgment on someone else, for at whatever*
> *point you judge another, you are condemning*
> *yourself, because you who pass judgment do*
> *the same things.* Romans 2 v 1

We may not look at porn, but which of us could say we are sexually pure? At the very least, have we never looked at someone else with lust in our hearts? We're all sinners, and we're all sexual sinners.

You may well, of course, be painfully aware of that fact—and reading this book has made you more conscious of it. You've been confronted, not only by the ugliness of porn, but by the ugliness of your own heart, mind and imagination, which have been sullied by what you've seen and read. You don't need convincing of your guilt—it burns within you.

God never responds to our sin by belittling it, as we are inclined to do. He doesn't say, *Don't worry, everyone does it. You're only human; it's no big deal.* The Bible says:

> *God is light and in him is no darkness at all.*
> *1 John 1 v 15*

He is the God of absolute moral perfection, who loves what is good, and who hates what is wicked and gets angry when he sees it.

Bobby Moore was the England soccer captain who received the World Cup from Queen Elizabeth when England won the trophy in 1966. An interviewer later asked him to describe how he felt. He talked of how terrified he was as he approached Her Majesty, because he noticed that she was wearing white gloves, while his hand, which would soon shake the Queen's, was covered in mud from the pitch. I have seen the footage of that scene many times. As the triumphant captain walks along the balcony, he keeps wiping his hand on his shorts, and then on the velvet cloth in front of the Royal box in a desperate attempt to get himself clean.

If Bobby Moore was worried about approaching the Queen with his muddy hands, how much more horrified should we be at the prospect of approaching God? Because of our sin, we are not just dirty on the outside; our hearts are unclean. And God doesn't just wear white gloves; he is absolutely pure, through and through. By ourselves, none of us can hope to approach him and live. And there's nothing we can do to make ourselves clean. But wonderfully, what we can't do, Christ has done for us.

## AN AMAZING SWAP

In his great love, God sent his Son, Jesus, to be our Saviour. Jesus was like us in every way, but without sin. He lived an absolutely perfect life, which included a perfect sexual life. He never looked at anyone lustfully. He always took his feelings to his heavenly Father in prayer, and did not go seeking alternative cures—even when he was under extreme pressure and hostility. He walked in the light, and never in darkness. And so he is the one person who ever lived who deserves relationship with God his Father.

But on the cross darkness descended. A spiritual darkness was symbolized by the gloom that covered Golgotha, the place where Jesus died. He was experiencing the awfulness of separation from his Father, not because of anything he had done, but because he was standing in for us. He took upon himself the punishment for our sins—all of them, even the most shameful, so that if we trust in him, we can be sure we've been forgiven.

Paul wrote to some Christians in the ancient city of Corinth, which had a reputation for debauchery, and he lists some of the sins they'd been engaged in, including sexual sin:

> *Do you not know that wrongdoers will not inherit the kingdom of God? Do not be deceived: neither the sexually immoral nor*

> *idolaters nor adulterers nor men who have*
> *sex with men nor thieves nor the greedy nor*
> *drunkards nor slanderers nor swindlers will*
> *inherit the kingdom of God.*
>
> 1 Corinthians 6 v 9-10

If he left it at that, there would be no hope for any of us. But, wonderfully, he continues:

> *And that is what some of you were. But you*
> *were washed, you were sanctified, you were*
> *justified in the name of the Lord Jesus Christ*
> *and by the Spirit of our God.*
>
> 1 Corinthians 6 v 9-11

Isn't that amazing? Those words apply to all of us who have trusted in Christ. "You were washed." We may go looking for that brain bath, and find ourselves washing ourselves in filth which leaves us feeling so dirty. But Jesus has washed us—we are perfectly clean in his sight, whatever sin we may have committed.

Paul also says this:

> *God made him who had no sin to be sin*
> *for us, so that in him we might become the*
> *righteousness of God.* 2 Corinthians 5 v 21

Tim Chester puts it well, applying those words to the sin of porn use:

*God made Jesus, who never looked with lust, to be a porn addict for us, so that in him we might become sexually pure.*[29]

The same could be said of every sexual sin that may be on our conscience: fantasising, looking at porn (however extreme the images may have been), sexting, sexual chat online, going too far physically outside of marriage, one-night stands, anonymous hookups, adulterous affairs, using prostitutes. These things are all on a continuum. The more we give in to one kind of sexual sin, the more likely it is we'll be pulled on to the next step… and the next.

You may feel you've already gone too far. You assume that other people would turn away from you in disgust if they knew what you've done. But, however others react, you need to grasp this amazing truth: *God did not turn away from you.* He sent his Son to die for you. Jesus took the penalty for all the filth of our sins so that they've all been dealt with— even those we haven't yet committed. Through Christ we are perfectly clean in God's sight. As the apostle John writes:

*The blood of Jesus, [God's] Son, purifies us from all sin.*　　　　　　　　1 John 1 v 7

---

29 *Captured by a Better Vision*, p 81.

## SAINTS, NOT SINNERS

An absolutely central part of Christian discipleship involves understanding and accepting who we really are; only then will we begin to live accordingly. The devil tries to drag us down: *What are you doing in church? How dare you presume to approach God in prayer after what you looked at last week! You should slink away in shame. You're a filthy sinner!*

The more we listen to those accusing words, the more likely we are to shy away from God and keep returning to our sin, but God has a very different message for us.

Of course, God knows that we continue to sin but, from the moment we turned to Christ, our sins no longer defined us. We've been united to Christ in his death and resurrection, and so we have a new identity. As Paul writes:

> *If anyone is in Christ, the new creation has come: the old has gone, the new is here!*
>
> 2 Corinthians 5 v 17

God sees us as if we were Jesus, without any stain of sin. That's why one of the most common words to describe Christians in the New Testament is "saints".[30] "Saint" is not a word that is only used to describe

---

30 E.g. Ephesians 1 v 1—the word is translated as "God's holy people" in the NIV 2011.

VAUGHAN ROBERTS

especially godly people; it speaks of all Christians, who have been made holy through Christ.

And so God says to us, even when we have fallen into sin and feel so ashamed, *You're perfect in my sight. You're a saint!*

## NEW HEARTS

Sin is an internal problem and it therefore demands an internal solution. That's why it's truly marvellous to know that our new identity as saints is not just a declaration by God of our new status in his sight—wonderful as that is—but that it goes even deeper. When Peter preached the gospel at Pentecost, he concluded:

> *Repent and be baptised, every one of you, in the name of Jesus Christ for the forgiveness of your sins. And you will receive the gift of the Holy Spirit.* Acts 2 v 38

The Christian message isn't simply, *You'll be forgiven if you trust in Jesus and then one day, after Jesus returns, you'll be perfect, but in the meantime, you can't expect to change very much.* Yes, when we put our trust in Jesus, we are completely forgiven, but there's another amazing promise as well. We also receive the Holy Spirit, who transforms us from within, giving us a new heart with new desires, so we should expect to change and become more holy.

It is true that the old nature lives on and keeps dragging us down, which is why we sin. But those who know Christ don't respond by thinking to themselves, "I'm glad I did that". If you feel terrible when you do something wrong, like looking at porn, it's a good sign. That's the Holy Spirit at work. He has given us a new longing: to please Jesus and become more like him. And he doesn't only convict us of our sin; he also helps us root it out.

Perhaps you've made many resolutions in the past to stop looking at porn, but they've never lasted and you've always gone back to it. You may think there's no hope, but that is a lie of the devil. You *can* change![31] You're not on your own in the battle against porn.

It's true that we'll never be perfect in this present world, but with the help of the Holy Spirit, we can and should expect transformation so that we increasingly grow in holiness.

## "THE NEW WAY OF THE SPIRIT"

If we feel that, despite our efforts, there has been little or no change in our behaviour, could it be that

---

31 See Tim Chester's excellent book *You can Change: God's Transforming Power for our Sinful Behaviour and Negative Emotions* (IVP, 2008).

we've been going about it in the wrong way? Paul writes:

> *We serve in the new way of the Spirit, not in*
> *the old way of the written code.*
>
> Romans 7 v 6

"The old way of the written code" speaks of the way that people under the old covenant sought to please God by trying to live up to a set of external standards, written on tablets of stone, by their own efforts. It was a hopeless quest, because their hearts remained cold towards God. But, wonderfully, we don't have to live like that any more. As those who have the Holy Spirit living in our hearts, we are called to live in "the new way of the Spirit". With his help we really can live porn-free lives.

We'll explore how in the final chapter.

# LIVING PORN FREE

## CHAPTER SIX

A young woman wrote to a pastor confessing that she had got "trapped in a web" of online pornography and masturbation:

> *I don't know who I am anymore. I am so scared ... I do what I know is wrong. I have tried to stop—really, I have. I have cried and sobbed at night. I have prayed and kept journals. I have read books. I am honestly at a loss. I love God, but I cannot continue to ask for forgiveness over and over and over for the same thing. I know I need help, but I don't know how to get it. I know that God has so much more planned for my life than this. But this sin continues to conquer me.*[32]

32 Josh Harris, *Sex Is Not the Problem (Lust Is)* (Multnomah, 2003) p 21-22.

You may be trying to help someone who has the same experience. Or perhaps you feel like that yourself. You long to get rid of porn, but you don't know how. If not, I'd be very surprised if you have never felt like that about some other sin.

I hope this chapter will give you hope and point you to a way out of the trap. Please read it together with the previous chapter—the two go together. Chapter 5 has laid out the foundations of what I want to say here. Through Christ, those who trust in him have already been set free from the guilt of porn by his death for them. And by the Holy Spirit, they have also been freed from the grip of porn. We don't have to keep going back to it, because we have the power of God living within us. But what does it mean in practice to live "in the new way of the Spirit" (Romans 7 v 6)?

## THE BATTLE WE ALL FACE

Inside every Christian there's a tug of war going on. The sinful nature (which the Bible calls "the flesh") still lingers. It tries to drag us into disobedience, egged on by its allies: the devil and the "world" (which means people who still live in opposition to God). But we now have a new nature which gives us a deep longing to please God.

Every time we experience temptation we have a

choice. We can either go the way of the sinful nature or "keep in step with the Spirit" (Galatians 5 v 25), living according to the new desires he gives us. What we do will depend on which of the two natures we are feeding. We are called to starve the old nature and to feed the new one. What that will look like in practice can be summed up in four brief phrases:

- Keep looking to Christ
- Trust in God's promises
- Be ruthless with sin
- Never give up

## KEEP LOOKING TO CHRIST

Take a moment to remember the times in your life when you *didn't* feel trapped by sin and grew most in holiness. Why was that?

I'd be very surprised indeed if it wasn't a period when you were bowled over by God's love for you in Christ and thrilled with the wonder of the gospel. That was the work of the Holy Spirit in you. He doesn't draw attention to himself; his great delight is to point people to Christ so that they grow in knowledge and love of him. As Jesus said, speaking of the Spirit's ministry, "He will glorify me" (John 16 v 14).

I heard once of a teenager who spent hours everyday gaming on his computer. His parents used threats and punishments to try to make him change his behaviour, but nothing really worked. But then they began to notice that he had completely lost interest in the games that used to consume so much of his time. *Why?* He'd met a girl, and, compared to her, his old habit had become unattractive.

Something similar happens as the Holy Spirit opens our eyes to see the beauty of Christ. So, if we want to fight against porn, or any other wrong behaviour, we shouldn't just focus on the sin and try to beat it out of our lives. That won't achieve much. We should, rather, focus not on our sin, but on what the Bible tells us about our Saviour.

As we grow in appreciation of who Christ is and what he has done for us, we will find our desire to fight sin and pursue holiness will grow. That may begin with a deeper conviction of sin. Too often we hardly care about our repeated patterns of wrong behaviour. Perhaps we've looked at those images or indulged those fantasies so often and for so long that it has become normal and we think little of it. But surely that must change as our hearts are melted by the gospel once more.

We need to heed the advice of John Owen, the 17th-century English Puritan. He wrote:

> *Bring thy lust to the gospel—not for relief [yet] but for farther conviction of its guilt … Say to*

*thy soul, "What have I done? What love, what mercy, what blood, what grace have I despised and trampled on! Is this the return I make to the Father for his love, to the Son for his blood, to the Holy Spirit for his grace? ... Have I defiled the heart that Christ died to wash, that the blessed Spirit has chosen to dwell in?* [33]

It's not that sin is impossible for a Christian who has received the Spirit—sadly not—but it should be unthinkable. One man who had kept going back to porn described the truth that had made a decisive difference:

*However much I tried it, the will power of "just don't look at it" never worked. I could go for a few days, and then the hole left just had to be filled. But then God made me realise that my choice was not simply between sinning or not. It was between desiring Jesus, who would satisfy, or desiring something else which wouldn't. The struggle didn't become easy then, but it did become winnable, because I realised I had to choose, not to walk away from*

---

33 Quoted in Tim Keller, "Puritan Resources for Biblical Counseling", Christian Counseling and Education Foundation (website), 1 June 2010. Accessed 9 May 2017.

*something, but towards someone.* [34]

So, fighting sin is not, first and foremost, about what we say no to. That "no" must always follow our "yes" to Jesus Christ, who has already said an amazing "*YES*" to us. As Heath Lambert writes:

> *You need to be the kind of person who fights for a close relationship with Jesus more than you fight against pornography … When you find yourself working to look to Christ more than you find yourself working to avoid porn, you'll know you've turned the corner … A living, breathing relationship with Jesus will drive porn out of your life quicker than anything else. When you turn your eyes to Jesus, there isn't room for anything else in your heart because he fills it up.*[35]

So how is our relationship with Jesus? Is he at the centre of our Christian lives, or have we begun to focus on other things? Have we got into the habit of reading the Bible day by day? If so, that will be a great help, but we need to remember that it's not a textbook of theology; it's a relational book through which God is drawing us into a deeper knowledge of himself.

---

34 Julian Hardyman, *Idols: God's Battle for our Hearts* (IVP, 2010), p 58-59.

35 *Finally Free* (Zondervan, 2013), p144.

Turn to it as a love letter from Jesus, and ask the Holy Spirit to enable you to meet him as you read. And it would also be good to pray as you go to church meetings that the Spirit would open your heart so that you're not just going through the motions. Ask him to help you engage deeply with God as you listen to his word, pray to him, sing his praises and meet his people. Of course we won't always feel especially close to Christ but, as with any relationship, we can expect growth in intimacy as we persevere.

## TRUST IN GOD'S PROMISES

The Bible is "the sword of the Spirit" (Ephesians 6 v 17). So, if we are to live in "the new way of the Spirit", it is vital that we keep turning to God's word, through preaching, in groups and in our own personal reading. One of the chief works of the Spirit is to help us understand, appreciate and trust in God's word. As we read it, we should pay special attention to the many glorious promises it contains, which will be a great help as we fight against sin. Here are just a few:

> *There is now no condemnation for those who are in Christ Jesus.*　　　　　Romans 8 v 1

Satan delights to make us wallow in the guilt of our sin, so that we feel far from Christ and are therefore much more vulnerable to further temptation. But you can banish the devil by reminding him and yourself of this great truth: *Christ has already paid the penalty for your sin, so you don't have to.*

You will feel guilty after you've fallen back into sin and yes, what you did was wrong and you shouldn't have done it. But however you feel, that doesn't change the glorious fact that you are absolutely secure in God's love. His acceptance of you doesn't depend on anything that you do or don't do, but on what Christ has already done for you. *Alleluia, what a Saviour!*

> *Whoever drinks the water I give them will*
> *never thirst.* John 4 v 14

Jesus spoke these words to the Samaritan woman who had been married five times and was now living with another man. It seems she had been looking to sexual relationships to bring satisfaction, but had never found it. And Jesus tells her, *I can give you what you're looking for.* He says the same to all of us. Porn promises much, but it never delivers; it can't give us the intimacy, self-worth or sense of control that we crave. But Jesus Christ meets the deepest longing of our hearts which, whether we recognise it or not, lies behind all the other desires: he alone can bring us into relationship with God. Only when we come to him, and keep coming, will our thirst be quenched.

*God is faithful; he will not let you be tempted beyond what you can bear. But when you are tempted, he will also provide a way out so that you can endure it.* 1 Corinthians 10 v 13

However powerful a particular temptation may be, God in his great faithfulness is still at work. He is by your side offering you a way of escape. So don't give up. Open the eyes of faith and take the exit path that God has provided. It could be a friend, ready to talk if you will only call, or some great truth you read about in the Bible just a few hours before, which you could bring to mind and heart. There is always a way out.

*Never will I leave you; never will I forsake you.* Hebrews 13 v 5

We are never on our own. Christ is with us by his Spirit every step of the way, ready to bring comfort or strength if we will only turn to him. He is always just a prayer away. Once we've started on the road to sin, we don't have to take the next step. He is right there with us, ready to help. And if we wilfully continue anyway and go down into the depths, he is still with us, waiting to pick us up. At that point it may feel that he is a million miles away, but he really isn't. So however you feel and whatever you've done, cling to this amazing promise and keep turning to

Christ in prayer, knowing that he always delights to hear you.

There are many other wonderful promises in the Bible. Why not write your favourites down and have them ready to turn to when you need them?

## BE RUTHLESS WITH SIN

We have seen that we will never win the fight against porn, or any other sin, if we seek to rely on resolutions and rules alone. The battle is won or lost in the heart.

But self-discipline still has a part to play. However close our walk with Christ, we remain vulnerable to temptation, and the more we have fallen in the past, the quicker it can happen again. So we will need to do all we can to protect ourselves where we are most vulnerable.

Jesus said, "If your right eye causes you to stumble, gouge it out" (Matthew 5 v 29). He wasn't speaking literally, of course, but his point is clear: we are to do whatever it takes to root sin out of our lives. Our tendency is to be much less radical, so we feel satisfied if we've reduced our sin to what we regard as a more acceptable level. But Paul wrote, "Among you there must not be even a hint of sexual immorality" (Ephesians 5 v 3). It's not enough to reduce the frequency of porn use or to shift to less explicit images; we're called to cut it out altogether.

What practical steps would you need to take to enable that to happen? I know friends who ensure that the family's computer is in a public place in the house, but that won't help with laptops or smart-phones. *Have you got the filters and accountability partners you need?* [36]

Having an accountability partner who also struggles with porn is unlikely to give you sufficient motivation to fight. Choose someone you respect and who can also point you to Jesus—a mature Christian, pastor or parent. Don't wait for them to ask the right question in the right way—the onus is on you to be honest and open. If you still find you can't stop, further steps may be necessary. Do you actually need internet on your phone? It's a great relief for me not to have it, not just because it removes temptations, but also because it frees up so much time.

*Are there particular times when temptation is most likely to strike?* If so, what else could you be doing then? Perhaps going out, listening to Christian music or phoning a friend would help. And if certain moods make us more vulnerable, how could we counter them?

Think of moods in terms of traffic-light colours. Green is when we feel calm and able to cope. Amber

---

36 See p 81 for websites that offer help with accountability.

or yellow is when we are beginning to feel under pressure and our mood is dipping, perhaps because we are feeling stressed, lonely or down. That can then lead to red, when those feelings are stronger.

Some find that sexual temptation is particularly intense in the red zone, because they've got used in the past to looking to porn to medicate these negative feelings. If so, they are likely to have been conscious of the temptation gradually mounting as they've moved from green towards red.

The further they go down that path, the louder the little voice in the head will be, telling them that only porn can make them feel better. So they need to take action early—before they get into the red zone.

That might involve talking to someone and asking for their prayers and encouragement. Sometimes just the very fact of having shared what we're feeling can reduce its intensity. Focusing on something else can also help—perhaps watching a movie, playing sport or having a meal with friends—anything to focus our minds on something else.

Above all of course, we should look to Christ and seek comfort from him. Sometimes nothing we do will prevent us from dipping into the red zone but, however we feel, we can be sure that he is still with us. Sin is never inevitable. The temptation may be very strong, but Jesus Christ is far stronger.

## NEVER GIVE UP

If you're still conscious of the pull of porn, I pray this short book has given you hope. Countless people have testified to how Jesus Christ has delivered them from porn, and you could join them. You don't have to keep going back to the false medicine it offers. If the approach I have described in these pages helps you move away from habitual sin, you need to remember that it certainly won't be the end of your battle against sin—or against sexual sin, which will keep appearing in other forms—so the fight will continue.

Perhaps reading this book has given you a renewed resolve to pursue holiness and greater hope that you can stop using porn. If so, that's great, but I need to warn you. It won't be easy and it's sadly likely that you will fall again. If you do, that's a key moment. The devil is bound to tell you, *It's no use—nothing has changed. You might as well give up—it's hopeless.* If you believe that lie, you'll soon be dragged back into the old pattern.

But there's another way. Quickly confess your sin and then move on. Don't wallow in the guilt or beat yourself up; that won't help. Turn to God's promise of forgiveness in Christ and step forward in faith with a joyful spring in your step. That's not taking your sin lightly; it's taking God's word seriously.

The battle against sin, in one form or another,

will continue throughout this present life. But we're called to press on, strengthened by the glorious promise that one day the struggle will be over and we'll be perfectly conformed to the likeness of Christ.[37] So, in the meantime, can I urge you brother, sister: *fight on*? The words of an old chorus, which meant so much to me when I was first converted, put it well:

> *Be valiant, be strong, resist the powers of sin;*
> *The fight is long, the foe is strong, but you*
>    *shall win.*
> *For through the power of Christ, the stronger*
>    *than the strong,*
> *You shall be more than conqueror;*
>    *Be valiant, be strong.*

---

37 See 1 John 3 v 2.

# HELPING OTHERS
## CHAPTER SEVEN

**S**ome of us will have particular responsibilities in helping others, whether to protect them from porn or to help them escape from its clutches. Individual situations will vary, but here are some general pointers as to how we can help.

## 1. HOW SHOULD I REACT WHEN A CHRISTIAN FRIEND TELLS ME THEY HAVE A PROBLEM WITH PORN?

It may be that your friend has never shared this with anyone before, so do thank them for their honesty and for placing their trust in you. Make sure you listen properly before offering any advice, and ask appropriate questions to help them share whatever they want to share (e.g. How long has this been going on? How often? Etc.).

Assuming they want to trust in Christ and to repent, assure them of God's forgiveness through the cross. They may feel dirty, but they are perfectly clean in God's sight.

## 2. HOW CAN I HELP MY FRIEND GET FREE OF PORN?

It's important to remember that you can't fix people —only God can do that. So don't take a huge burden of responsibility onto yourself, but turn to him in prayer. Then aim to help your friend understand and apply the principles I outlined in the previous chapter. Above all, that will mean pointing them to Christ and his gospel.

Do talk to your friend about practical ways in which they could place barriers on their access to porn (accountability filters etc.). Such measures have an important role, but don't focus on them. Nothing is more important in the battle against porn than a growing love for Christ and appreciation of all we have received in him.

That is true, of course, in the fight against *all* sin, and it's important to remind your friend not to focus on fighting porn alone, while ignoring other sins. You yourself may not look at porn, but you're a sinner too. Be open about *your* particular struggles, and look for a two-way encouragement to strive for holiness. Your sins may be different, but you both need the same remedy.

If you also have a problem with porn, it will be important that you are both open with another person. Choose someone who will hold you to high standards and point you always to Christ.

## 3. SHOULD I TELL MY SPOUSE IF I HAVE BEEN USING PORN?

We have already recognised that porn is very damaging to marriages (see p 35). If you are married and are using porn, you need to repent and seek all the help you can to stop. Both the sin itself, and the secrecy that goes with it, will damage intimacy and ultimately threaten your marriage.

So, if this has been or is a significant problem, your husband or wife needs to know about it. Wisdom is needed in deciding exactly how much detail is necessary in the confession. That judgment should be determined not by a selfish fear of exposure, but by a loving concern for your spouse and for what is best for your marriage. If your spouse asks for more detail, it should be given. The same principles apply to relationships between boy- and girl-friends, but how they are worked out will depend on the nature of the relationship—how serious the problem is, and how long you have been dating, etc.

## 4. HOW SHOULD I RESPOND IF I DISCOVER MY SPOUSE HAS BEEN USING PORN?

The revelation that your husband or wife has been using porn during your marriage will be very painful. Strong feelings of anger, hurt and rejection are understandable, but they should not govern how you respond. It may help to talk to a trusted friend as you seek God's wisdom to react appropriately. What that looks like will depend on the circumstances.

Assuming there has been genuine apology and repentance, there should always be forgiveness. But you will also want to be reassured that everything necessary is being done to prevent an ongoing pattern of sin. Some kind of accountability will be important, but you needn't be directly involved with it. It may be better for a friend or pastor to take the lead in this, but your spouse still needs to be open with you if there is a recurrence.

## 5. HOW CAN PARENTS PROTECT THEIR CHILDREN FROM PORN?

The sad reality is that while parents make every effort to protect their children, the likelihood is that they will be exposed to porn. It is a challenging world for young people to grow up in, but don't despair—there is much you can do to help them. Above all else, teach your children the Bible and pray they will grow up knowing and loving the Lord Jesus. Nothing is more effective in the fight against sin than a heart that loves Christ and longs to please him.

Aim to teach your children to know God and honour him in all of life. That should certainly include teaching about sex. Don't leave this to the church or school; aim for your voice to be the first they hear on the subject. And make sure the emphasis is positive. Sex in God's design is not dirty or shameful; it is his good gift for married couples.

In protecting your children against porn, you will need to explain why it is ugly and harmful. But don't rely on teaching alone. Your children are sinful and porn is everywhere, so don't be naive. Allowing them internet access on their phone or in the privacy of their own room without proper controls is like leaving them with a loaded gun.[38]

If they do watch porn, it's important that your children feel able to talk to you about it. Seek to cultivate a culture of confession in the home. Openness about sin, handling temptation and failure in general will make confession in this area easier. Your children need to know that if they admit to sin, they won't be met with shock and horror.

---

38 Advice on how to protect your children online can be found at protectyourkids.org.uk.

All parents will feel out of their depth at times. So do talk to fellow parents and others in your local church for advice and encouragement. And at all times, keep looking to the sovereign Lord. He has purposed for your children to be born in this age, so commit them daily to him with quiet confidence.

## 6. HOW CAN PASTORS HELP?

Before thinking about how we help others, we need to recognise that as pastors we are not immune from sexual sin ourselves. We need to ensure we do everything necessary to protect ourselves in areas where we are weak, and also seek help if we fall. If porn is a problem for you, it's vital that you tell someone and become accountable to them.

Pastors more than anyone else, under God, set the culture in a church. In our preaching we need to ensure the focus is always on Christ as we expound the Scriptures. The battle for holiness is won or lost in the heart, so we must pray that our church family grows together in an ever deeper delight in Christ and desire to live for him.

Church leaders are called to preach "the whole counsel of God" (Acts 20 v 27) from the Bible, and that must include teaching about sex. The world is bombarding our congregations with lies about sex all the time. It's vital that we don't respond with a coy silence, but teach God's truth without apology or embarrassment. Above all, the emphasis should be positive. Show the goodness of God's loving design for sex and marriage. When did you last preach a series—or even just one sermon—on this subject? [39]

While holding people to God's high standards, we should acknowledge publicly that we all fall short. Too many of our churches are marked by outward respectability and secret shame. This prevents openness about sin and leaves people trapped by it.

We also need to make conscious efforts to ensure that it is easier for members of our congregation to receive the help they need. The statistics indicate that in any given congregation, there may be up to a third of people present who are dabbling in porn, and some of them may be thoroughly in its grip. So how about adding a line or two in a sermon? "If you're struggling with some kind of sexual sin— perhaps porn—please don't let it be a lonely battle. I hope you'd feel able to talk to someone. We're all sinners…"

Arranging a practical seminar on helping people fight against porn could also bring the subject into the open. In our own church we have found *Celebrate*

---

39 I strongly recommend Glynn Harrison's book *A Better Story* as a model of how to teach positively on this subject in the contemporary world.

*Recovery*[40] has been a significant help to people facing a variety of "hurts, hangups, and habits", including porn. It has not only tended to draw those experiencing quite severe struggles, but the publicity for the group has also helped the church as a whole face up to weakness and vulnerability.

40 See John Baker, *Celebrate Recovery* (Zondervan, 2005) and celebraterecovery.co.uk.

## FURTHER RESOURCES

### Books

Stephen Arterburn, *Every Man's Battle* (Waterbrook Multnomah, 2009).

Tim Chester, *Captured by a Better Vision* (IVP, 2010).

Josh Harris, *Sex is Not the Problem (Lust is): Sexual Purity in a Lust-Saturated World* (Multnomah, 2005).

Heath Lambert, *Finally Free: Fighting for Purity with the Power of Grace* (Zondervan, 2013).

Helen Thorne, *Purity is Possible: How to Live Free of the Fantasy Trap* (The Good Book Company, 2014).

Tim Lane and Paul David Tripp, *How People Change* (New Growth Press, 2009).

Dai Hankey, *A Man's Greatest Challenge: How to Build Self-Control That Lasts* (The Good Book Company, 2014).

Glynn Harrison, *A Better Story* (IVP, 2017).

## Websites

www.covenanteyes.com—Christian accountability website

x3watch.com—Christian accountability website

dirtygirlsministries.com—Christian website with resources for women fighting sexual addiction

fightthenewdrug.org—A secular website which doesn't deal with the heart issue, but has helpful information about the damage porn does.

www.stopitnow.org.uk—A website that offers advice and help on child abuse, including a helpful downloadable booklet on how to talk to friends and family if you suspect they are involved in viewing child pornography, called *Let's Talk*.

## Parents and Children

Nicholas Black, *iSnooping on your Kid: Parenting in the Internet World* (New Growth, 2012).

Kristen Jenson, *Good Pictures Bad Pictures: Porn-Proofing Today's Young Kids* (Glen Cove Press, 2014). This is a book to read with your child.

Covenant Eyes has a section about how to protect your children online: protectyourkids.org.uk

## Acknowledgements

I am grateful to Luke Cornelius, Ian Fry, Lizzie Ling, Amy O'Donovan, Matt Pope and Sharon Wilmshurst for many helpful comments and suggestions as I was writing this book. Audrey Southgate did a great job in turning my dictations and untidy scrawl into a perfect typescript. Tim Thornborough has once more been all I could hope for in an editor.

# THE PORN PROBLEM
## DISCUSSION GUIDE

This series does not aim to say everything there is to say about a subject, but to give an overview and a solid grounding to Christians who are starting to think about the issue from the Bible. We hope that as you discuss this book, and the Bible passages that it is based on, you will gain confidence to speak faithfully, compassionately and wisely to others.

Below is a list of questions. Please pick and choose the ones that suit your group, and the time you have available. If you are leading a group, try to keep constantly in people's minds that this is not simply a discussion about a political or moral "issue"—but part of the way our whole society views and thinks about sexuality. How we think, react to, talk and teach about sexuality in general, and pornography in particular, will shape how well we relate to the wider non-Christian culture, and particularly to young people today.

## TO START

- We recognise that many people find pornography and sexuality difficult subjects to talk about. Is that a good thing or a bad thing? Why do we find these things so hard to talk about? What are some of the negative effects when Christians, perhaps for very good reasons, are silent on this subject, both in formal teaching in church and in conversations with others?

- What attitudes have you heard expressed about pornography from other people? What do you think are some of the positives and negatives in regard to each of these viewpoints?

- In what areas have you noticed the increase in sexual images or the acceptability of talking about sex in books, movies and advertising, and on TV and the radio? How do you think your standards have changed on these things over the years?

## CHAPTER 1: THE PORN PROBLEM

- If you are able to, talk about how pornography was regarded when you were young. What was your first experience of pornographic images or writing, and how did it make you feel?
- "Freedom" has been one of the driving forces to soften censorship of pornography in our culture. Where do you think this freedom will end? What kind of culture are we heading towards, do you think?

## CHAPTER 2: SEX AND GOD'S DESIGN

- *Thinking about sex.* Why do Christians find it difficult to talk openly about sex and sexuality?
- "Sex is not simply recreational; it is profoundly relational" (p 23). Do you agree? Would people who do not share your Christian convictions agree?
- How would you articulate the Christian view of our bodies and sex to someone who had never read the Bible? What would you be concerned to emphasise?
- If there was a national vote to end censorship completely, how do you think people would vote? What arguments might be put forward for and against the motion?
- What do you make of Paul's statement in Ephesians 5 v 32? How does it change our view of the ultimate purpose of sex in God's design?

## CHAPTER 3: THE UGLINESS OF PORN

Go through each of the statements in the chapter, and try to come up with examples and explanations for each of them. Have you experienced of the truth of these statements yourself? How would you articulate these viewpoints to a teenager or an adult?

- Porn cheapens sex
- Porn objectifies people
- Porn damages self-esteem
- Porn harms the young
- Porn corrupts its users
- Porn turns people in on themselves
- Porn undermines marriage
- Porn undermines future marriages

## CHAPTER 4: THE SLAVERY OF PORN

- Vaughan lists a number of root causes of porn addiction on page 42: *"Is it a longing for intimacy or control? What are you medicating? Is it low self-image—a sense that people are looking down on you so you feel small and unimportant? Or perhaps you feel that no one loves you—and porn seems to take those negative emotions away."* Do you find these reasons convincing? Are there any that you would want to add to the list?

- *Addiction* (p 44): Have you noticed any of the symptoms of addiction listed here, or seen them in others? How might you open a discussion about this with a friend or family member whom you suspect may be struggling with porn addiction?

## CHAPTER 5: TRUE FREEDOM

- We feel sexual sin very deeply in ourselves, and yet it is just one sin among many. Why and how is sexual sin the same as, and yet in some ways more serious than other sins? How do we find a right balance in thinking about and responding to sexual sin in ourselves and in others?
- God offers forgiveness and a fresh start for repentant sinners. What are the implications of 1 Corinthians 6 v 9-10 and 2 Corinthians 5 v 21 for ourselves, and for the way we welcome and encourage others?

## CHAPTER 6: LIVING PORN FREE

- Do you find the solutions offered in this chapter realistic?
- What examples of real change have you experienced in your own Christian walk?
- What things can a church family do to encourage both honesty with our individual struggles, and accountability which will help us strive for holiness?
- Which of the promises on pages 65-67 do you find especially encouraging or comforting? What other promises from God's word might you offer to someone who is wrestling with porn addiction?
- *Be ruthless with sin (p 68)*: What, in your experience, are the factors that cause you to give up in your fight against sin? What have you got in place to help you when those factors are pressing in on you?

## CHAPTER 7: HELPING OTHERS

- Which question is especially pertinent for you at the moment? Do you find the advice relevant? How would you extend or nuance the answer?

- A parent asks your advice about setting rules for the kind of TV programmes they should allow their children to watch, and how they should manage their child's use of the internet. What could you say?
- What question could be missing from the list? How might you answer it, having read this book?

## TO FINISH

- What's the big thing that has impacted you from reading *The Porn Problem*?
- How will you think about and pray for those who are tempted or ensnared by porn??
- What extra help and information do you think you need to be better equipped in discussing this issue with others, and in helping others to see how porn enslaves but Jesus brings freedom?

## PRAY

- Ask God to help you understand the issue and the people involved with it better.
- Pray that your church fellowship would be a place where people find the freedom to talk about their struggles with this so-often secret issue. Pray that they would be taught, supported and encouraged in their struggle with sin.
- Pray for parents and children in your church. Ask God to guide them as they seek to navigate these difficult waters.

Printable copies of this discussion guide are available at:
www.thegoodbook.co.uk/the-porn-problem
www.thegoodbook.com/the-porn-problem

A TALKING POINTS BOOK BY
**VAUGHAN ROBERTS**

# TRANSGENDER

There's been huge cultural change in the last few decades. Same-sex marriage would have been unthinkable 20 or 30 years ago. Now it's almost universally accepted in the Western world. Suddenly the issue of transgender is the next big social, cultural issue that is dominating the headlines.

Vaughan Roberts surveys the Christian worldview and seeks to apply the principles he uncovers to the many complex questions surrounding gender identity. This short book gives an overview and a starting point for constructive discussion as we seek to live in a world with different values, and to love, serve and relate to transgender people.

Talking Points is a series of short books designed to help Christians think and talk about today's big issues, and to relate to others with compassion, conviction and wisdom.

*"In this brief book on a complex subject Vaughan Roberts combines the traditional Christian understanding of gender and the body with a very careful, loving, understanding stance toward transgender people. The two almost never go together, and that's why this book is so good!"*

Tim Keller, pastor, author and Vice-President of The Gospel Coalition

A TALKING POINTS BOOK BY
**VAUGHAN ROBERTS**

# ASSISTED DYING

There is a growing movement in many parts of the world to legalise assisted suicide: allowing doctors to help end someone's life if they so desire. What are Christians supposed to think about this issue, and how do we talk about it, and face these issues personally?

In this short book, Vaughan Roberts briefs Christians on the complex questions surrounding assisted suicide and the choices we face at the end of our lives. He surveys the Christian worldview and helps us to apply its principles as we navigate life and death in a society with contrasting values.

Talking Points is a series of short books designed to help Christians think and talk about today's big issues, and to relate to others with compassion, conviction and wisdom.

*"This little book is a very helpful resource for anyone coming to consider the difficult question of the place of human choice at the end of life for the first time. With a tone both sensitive and authentic in its shaping by personal experience, Roberts offers an erudite yet accessible survey of an issue set only to increase in significance."*
Andrew Moore, Apologist for the Zacharias Trust and Director of the RZIM Festival of Thought

thegoodbook.co.uk | thegoodbook.com
thegoodbook.com.au | thegoodbook.co.nz

**the good book**
## COMPANY

**BIBLICAL | RELEVANT | ACCESSIBLE**

At The Good Book Company, we are dedicated to helping Christians and local churches grow. We believe that God's growth process always starts with hearing clearly what he has said to us through his timeless word—the Bible.

Ever since we opened our doors in 1991, we have been striving to produce resources that honour God in the way the Bible is used. We have grown to become an international provider of user-friendly resources to the Christian community, with believers of all backgrounds and denominations using our Bible studies, books, evangelistic resources, DVD-based courses and training events.

We want to equip ordinary Christians to live for Christ day by day, and churches to grow in their knowledge of God, their love for one another, and the effectiveness of their outreach.

Call us for a discussion of your needs or visit one of our local websites for more information on the resources and services we provide.

Your friends at The Good Book Company

---

**UK & EUROPE**       thegoodbook.co.uk       0333 123 0880
**NORTH AMERICA**    thegoodbook.com           866 244 2165
**AUSTRALIA**        thegoodbook.com.au        (02) 9564 3555
**NEW ZEALAND**      thegoodbook.co.nz         (+64) 3 343 2463

 **WWW.CHRISTIANITYEXPLORED.ORG**
Our partner site is a great place for those exploring the Christian faith, with a clear explanation of the good news, powerful testimonies and answers to difficult questions.